STEVE WRIGHT'S
BOOK OF
FACTOIDS

HarperCollins*Entertainment*
An Imprint of HarperCollins*Publishers*
77–85 Fulham Palace Road,
Hammersmith, London W6 8JB

www.harpercollins.co.uk

Published by HarperCollins*Entertainment* 2005
3

Editor: Chris Smith
Design: Gary Day-Ellison

A CIP catalogue record for this book
is available from the British Library

ISBN 0 00 720660 7

Printed and bound in Belgium by Proost

STEVE WRIGHT'S
BOOK OF
FACTOIDS

Steve Wright

with Jessica Rickson

HarperCollins*Entertainment*
An Imprint of HarperCollins*Publishers*

STEVE WRIGHT'S
BOOK OF
FACTOIDS

Just when you thought it was Newport, the most common place name in Britain is Newtown, which occurs 150 times. *And the most common name for a shopping centre is Arndale – which is also my Uncle Len's middle name.*

The herring is the most widely eaten fish in the world. *Although not in itself very wide – in fact it's very flat and no fun whatsoever.*

Did you know that most COWS produce more milk when they listen to music? *Favourite with our bovine buddies are the Scissor Sisters and any oldie by Paul Young.*

Were you aware that Queen bees lay nearly 1,500 eggs a day and live for up to two years?

According to top space scientists, about **1,000** tons of space material enters the atmosphere every year and makes its way to the Earth's surface.

The world's deadliest recorded earthquake hit in central China in 1557, killing **830,000** people. In 1976, another tremor killed more than 250,000 people in Tangshan, China.

Apart from Croydon, the wettest place on Earth is Lloro, Colombia, which averages 523.6in of rainfall a year, or more than 40ft (13 metres). That's about 10 times more than the big cities in Europe.

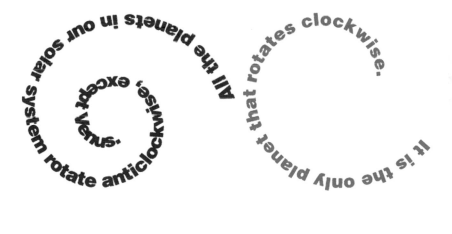

All the planets in our solar system rotate anticlockwise, except Venus. It is the only planet that rotates clockwise.

The **cockroach** is the fastest animal on six legs – covering a metre a second. *A little known extra factoid is that sizeable numbers of cockroaches have bad breath, and ... don't wash behind their ears.*

The whip makes a cracking sound because its tip moves faster than the speed of sound. *Oh – more! I'll have what she's having.*

Didaskaleinophobia is the fear of going to school.

One in four married women have a younger partner, like Madonna. *When Madonna married Guy Ritchie, he was only 18. She was 74.*

Electricity doesn't move through a wire but through a field around the wire.

The dot over the letter **" i "** is called a tittle.

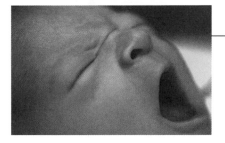

55 per cent of people yawn within five minutes of seeing someone else yawn. Reading about yawning makes most people yawn. *And yawning about Reading is against the law in Berkshire.*

An ostrich's **eye** is bigger than its brain. *They bury their heads in the sand to worry about this factoid.*

The recording artist with the most number one records is Elvis Presley – with 18 over 45 years.

Almonds are members of the **peach** family. *You remember the peach family – you looked after their fish when they were on holiday.*

Kylie Minogue is the most groped waxwork at Madame Tussauds.

Singer **Jamelia** recorded the demo tape that was to lead to her first record deal, on a toy karaoke machine.

Former racing driver Damon Hill played guitar in a punk band called Sex Hitler and the Hormones.

Ringo Starr was the first person in Britain to own a video recorder.

Love Actually star **Bill Nighy** suffers from Dupuytren's Contracture, which keeps the little and ring finger of each hand permanently bent back against the palm.

When she was eight, round the world yachtswoman **Ellen MacArthur** started saving her dinner money to buy a boat.

Rolling Stones star **Keith Richards** has a child called Dandelion.

Big-time actor **Colin Farrell** auditioned for boy-band Boyzone but was rejected by manager Louis Walsh because he couldn't sing.

Ozzy Osbourne was banned from Texas for ten years after being caught urinating on the revered Alamo fort in San Antonio. He was wearing a dress at the time.

Hilary Clinton became the first First Lady to win a Grammy when she won the gong for the Best Spoken Word album in 1996.

Arnold Schwarzenegger spoke only 700 words during the whole of the film, *The Terminator*. That worked out at £12,000 per word, almost double the £6,500 payment he received for his first film, *Hercules in New York*.

Martin Freeman, who played Tim in *The Office*, was in the England squash squad as a junior.

Ground Force presenter **Charlie Dimmock** wears a 36B bra. *Sometimes*.

R&B soul babe **Joss Stone** recorded her million-selling debut album – *The Soul Sessions* – in only four days.

Demi Moore was born cross-eyed.
...Is that why she can't see how young Ashton Kutcher is?

Victoria Beckham once admitted that she has never read a book from cover to cover.

Swedish supergroup **Abba** were originally called 'The Engaged Couples', **Oasis** was formerly known as 'Rain', **The Red Hot Chili Peppers** once called themselves 'Tony Flow and the Miraculous Majestic Masters of Mayhem', whilst **U2** initially performed as 'Feedback'.

Elvis Costello's father sang 'I'm a Secret Lemonade Drinker' on the advert for R White's Lemonade.

Anastacia owns 20 pairs of her trademark glasses.

Jemima Khan has developed her own brand of ketchup.

EastEnders Pat Butcher, actress **Pam St Clement**, has 125 pairs of earrings to choose from.

Before he became an actor, *Kumars at No 42* star **Sanjeev Bhaskar** completed a business degree and worked as a marketing manager for IBM. *He also married his own TV grandma.*

Before having a gastric band fitted to shrink her stomach, **Sharon Osbourne** used to weigh 16 stone. She is now half that weight. *A gastric band? We're not sure if* **Ozzy** *used to be in it.*

Johnny Vegas reportedly attended interviews and was accepted by the priesthood – he changed his mind at the last minute.

It was rumoured that during the filming of *American Idol*, judge **Paula Abdul** hired the services of a scriptwriter to come up with witty one-liners, which she could use to respond to attacks from judge **Simon Cowell**.

Desperate Housewives star **Eva Longoria** has a huge cross tattoo on her back. Producers of the show have to spend thousands of dollars digitally airbrushing it out when she is seen walking around in her underwear.

Tom Baker has been the longest serving Doctor Who, playing the part for seven years. His famous scarf was much longer than was originally planned, because its designer thought that all the coloured balls of wool provided had to be used.

Back with *Desperate Housewives*, **Nicollette Sheridan** is naturally a redhead but has been dying her hair blonde since she was 13 years old.

Robbie Williams is an ordained minister after completing a form online, which allowed him to officiate at a friend's wedding.

Celebrity section 1

15

Cold Feet and *My Dad's The Prime Minister* star Robert Bathhurst once auditioned for the role of James Bond.

When **Shane Richie** started out in showbusiness he was known by the stage name "Shane Skywalker". It was **Lenny Henry** who persuaded him to change it.

A recent opinion poll revealed that seventy per cent of people do not know which Geordie presenter is Ant and which is Dec.

Friends star **Matthew Perry** is missing part of the middle finger on his right hand.

When Julie Walters announced she was going to become an actress, her disappointed mum declared "she will be in the gutter before she's twenty".

Celebrity Section 1

Vanessa Feltz's first kiss was with dance DJ Pete Tong.

Simon Cowell and **Pete Waterman** were originally asked to come up with a theme tune for *Who Wants to Be a Millionaire*. Unfortunately the pair argued so much during initial meetings that the job was eventually given to someone else.

Liz Hurley auditioned for the role of Cassandra in *Only Fools and Horses*.

Gwyneth Paltrow wears size 9 shoes, whilst **Uma Thurman** wears a massive size 11

A goldfish has a memory span of three seconds. *Mmm, what? Who are you?*

Psycho was the first Hollywood film to show a toilet flushing and that generated many **complaints**. *The stabbing in the shower scene was okay, then?*

"Stewardesses" is the longest English word that is typed with only the left hand. *And I'll be back with your peanuts in a minute sir.*

The only **15-letter** word that can be spelled without repeating a letter is "uncopyrightable".

The greatest football headline ever written is said to be the one in *The Sun* in February 2000 after Inverness Caledonian Thistle beat Celtic 3-1 in the Scottish Cup:

"Super Caley Go Ballistic, Celtic Are Atrocious".

Thirty-one different shapes of UFO have been sighted, including the traditional saucer-shaped one. *Elvis was on board two of them.*

In the Stone Age half of all people were **left-handed**, but today only five per cent of us are left-handed. *Barney Rubble was himself left-handed.*

It is impossible to **lick** your elbow. *Please don't try, I was in Outpatients for 2½ days.*

After his first concert appearance, Elvis Presley **was advised to consider becoming a lorry driver.**
…Because he already looked like one.

The practice of "giving away the bride" goes back to the time when money exchanged hands for the privilege.

The very first episode of *Doctor Who* was shown on November 23, 1963 – the day after President Kennedy was assassinated. The nation was so shocked the show went unnoticed, so the BBC repeated it a week later.

It takes a lobster seven years to reach a weight of 500 grams.
Unless it dies screaming in a pot of boiling water.

The hair on your head grows at a rate of 0.34 millimetres a day. *But not on mine.*

The average two year old learns **16** new words a day. *Including "Are we there yet?"*

A can of Spam is opened every four seconds. *And it's getting fed up with it.*

A hippo can open its mouth wide enough to fit Little Ant and Dec inside.

Every time you lick a stamp, you're consuming 0.1 of a calorie. *So don't do it.*

If you add half a glass of **lemonade** to a vase of flowers, the bubbles prolong the life of the flowers by up to a week. *Bet you didn't know your flowers are secret lemonade drinkers.*

Despite her Essex girl image, blonde glamour model and party girl **Jodie Marsh** has 11 GCSEs and 3 A Levels.

22-year-old **Michael Carroll**, known as the King of Chavs, who won £9.7 million on the lottery in 2002, was given an anti- social behaviour order (**ASBO**) after admitting criminal damage by firing ball bearings from a catapult at cars and windows.

The word chav came from the Romany term "chavi", meaning child.

Hell's Kitchen winner **Jennifer Ellison** had elocution lessons before appearing in *Phantom of the Opera*, after Hollywood bosses struggled to understand her Scouse accent.

Jordan (aka Katie Price) once auditioned for a role in *Baywatch*. She was turned down.

In TV's chav-tastic *Celebrity Love Island*, when *Playboy* model **Nikki Ziering** arrived, one of **Paul Danan**'s first questions was to ask her how **Jennifer Aniston, Cameron Diaz** and **Justin Timberlake** were doing.

EastEnders star **Jessie Wallace** used to be a make-up artist and made up fellow *EastEnders* actor **Nigel Harman** when he was in the cast of **Abba** musical *Mamma Mia*.

After a newspaper reported that footballer **Wayne Rooney**'s fiancee **Coleen McLoughlin** had discarded her £25,000 engagement ring at the Formby Point Nature Reserve near the couple's luxury home, members of the pulic searching for the ring were banned from the reserve by the National Trust in case they disturbed the squirrels there.

A student at Leeds Metropolitan University wrote a 10,000 word thesis on "**chav-ology**" as part of her media studies degree. It was entitled "*Chavs – subculture or chavaphobia?*"

Chav extra factoid . . . "Popney" rhyming slang includes **Jay Kay** for takeaway, **Sinead O'Connor** for doner, **Fatboy Slim** for gym and **Noel Gallagher** for a week in Malaga.

The Earth is not round – it's actually slightly pear-shaped.
We all thought it went pear-shaped years ago.

American composer John Cage created a piece entitled
"4 minutes 33 seconds" *which is totally silent. That's just stupid!*

There were always 56 curls in 40s child starlet Shirley Temple's hair.

Most adults have between two and five colds a year.
Toddlers have between four and eight.

No matter how low the temperature falls outside, the windows
of an empty house never frost over. *Unless you know different . . .*

While he was Prince Regent, George VI used to maintain a pale, elegant appearance by being frequently bled.

Were you aware that when a female fish sees a male fish blowing bubbles, It means he's ready for breeding?

81% of people trust their partner to buy a surprise birthday present they will really like. *But what about the other 19%?*

It's a factoid that the first hard hats were worn by workers building the Vatican, but in which century was it:

   a) in the late 16th century

   b) in the late 18th century

   c) in the late 20th century

[Answer: a) in the late 16th century.]

Petersham is a *thick* corded silk ribbon used for stiffening in dressmaking. *So it's not a town in Surrey, then?*

Jane Austen included only 14 kisses in her novels altogether, and four of those were on the hand.

The average debt of students graduating in the summer of 2005 was £13,500 – more than 10 per cent up on 2004.

Residents in Newtown, Powys, Wales started a campaign to change their town's name as it was shared by more than 100 others.

Actor **Leonardo DiCaprio** has bought his own island in the Caribbean to turn into a five-star resort for wealthy conservation lovers.

If you're over 100 years old, there's an 80 per cent chance you're a woman. *You look good for your age – are those your own teeth?*

A nightclub in Somerset held its Christmas party in July so that fire crews, the ambulance service and hospital workers could come.

Elephants are the only animals that can't jump. *Well, have you ever seen one do it? Are they ever in the Olympics? Well then!*

There are officially 193 countries in the world, alphabetically from Afghanistan to Zimbabwe.

Peter Sellers' film contracts used to stipulate that he had to be supplied with a bed pointing East-West. So that he could clearly see Leytonstone from where he was lying ...

Such is the popularity of footballer **David Beckham** that when he revealed a hairless chest during a summer sunbathing session while on holiday in St Tropez, sales of home waxing kits soared.

Eskimos complained of a heatwave when the temperature in the Arctic soared to 19 degrees Centigrade ... *Suppose their igloos melted all over their pyjamas ...*

A magician had to pay a locksmith £130 to free him after he got trapped in handcuffs when a trick on stage went wrong. *Muppetry*.

After bad reviews for his early films, **Harrison** "Indiana Jones" **Ford** gave up acting to become a carpenter. *But please, no jokes about his acting being wooden – Harrison is a fine actor ... and a very good friend.*

The most impossible item to flush down a toilet is a ping-pong ball, *but obviously the researchers have never tried an elephant.*

 Maria Sharapova, the 2004 Wimbledon tennis champion, turned up at the following year's event with 10 pairs of £500 trainers, flecked with 24-carat gold.

Between shows, **Elvis** used to **snack** on chicken soup with crackers.
As the crowd called "More!" he ate more.

It's **reported** that when **Elvis** was introduced to Eric Clapton, he said to Slow Hand "And what do you do?"

Elvis impersonators are officially known as "Elvii" – just Ask Elvis. *And don't they say that by the year* **2080**, *every other citizen will be an Elvis impersonator?*

Elvis **bought** hundreds of silk scarves to throw to fans at his shows, *mainly from Tie Rack on Victoria Station.*

The most successful music act of all time is **Elvis Presley**, having spent nearly 2,500 weeks in the UK charts alone.

RCA, the record label **Elvis** was on, always had to use the pressing plants of other **record** labels right from his first song with them to keep up with demand.

Elvis used to always call his **daughter** Lisa-Marie "Buttonhead" or "Yisa".

Graceland is the second most visited home in America, after the White House. He bought Graceland for $102,500 in March 1957.
Well, do you know how much it's worth now ...?

You could only enter **Elvis**'s bathroom with his permission. *It boasted a padded toilet, a poster of Sarah Kennedy and a giant Blue Peter badge. That's not widely known – keep it to yourself.*

Nobody apart from the British royal family has appeared on the **stamps** of more countries than **Elvis**.

Elvis wore high turned up collars because he believed his neck was too long, and he never wore **underpants**. *In fact, his collars were named after two giraffes at Memphis Zoo, and he could never find underpants in his size, and he found them restrictive.*

Elvis has left the building.

Less than seven per cent of the population donates blood.

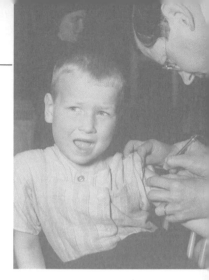

Forty per cent of women have hurled what at a man?

- a) abuse
- b) drink
- c) footwear

[If it was a) or b) I'm sure the figure would be higher, but it's actually c) footwear. Clearly our better halves not only like to shop for them they like to throw them as well.]

In Japan, 20% of all publications sold are comic books.

The odds of being killed by falling out of bed are one in two million.

After a concert on the Isle of Man, the Rolling Stones climbed through a toilet window to avoid screaming fans.

Chart anorak factoid, courtesy of Paul Gambaccini – In 1976, Rodrigo's 'Guitar Concerto de Aranjuez' was No 1 in the UK for only three hours because of a computer error.

200 babies are born worldwide every minute.

One out of every 70 people who pick their nose eat what they find! *That is sick! Get help.*

43 per cent of men speak to their mums on the telephone at least once a week.

There are no **clocks** in Las Vegas gambling casinos.

90 per cent of women who walk into a department store immediately turn to the right.

Walking fast uses *eight* times as many calories as writing. *Especially when you're carrying a tortoise.*

31

A study has revealed that people are more likely to catch colds when their mothers-in-law come to stay – too much stress brings down their immune system.

The tranquiliser Valium is the most widely used drug on earth.

In the native Indian language Manhattan means "the place of drunkenness".

One count of the word "and" in the Bible showed that it appears 46,227 times.

14 per cent of cat owners think their cat is more important than their job.

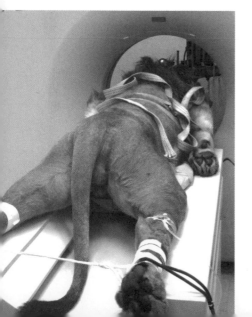

The lion has the smallest heart of all beasts of prey.

The *shark* is immune to all known diseases.

The frog's tongue grows from the front of its mouth,
which makes it easier to catch flies.

People in Southern England eat six million more cloves of
garlic a year than the northern French.

Red-haired men are more likely to go bald than anyone else.

A foetus acquires fingerprints at the age of:

 a) 3 weeks
 b) 3 months
 c) 9 months

[Answer: b) three months.]

**Three-quarters of the world's population
wash from top to bottom in the shower.**

More money is spent on gardening
than on any other hobby.

£25,000 is the highest price
paid for a donkey in the UK.
The prized beast was a racing
donkey called Minstrel.

Many sailors believe a cat on board a ship means:

a) a lucky trip

b) an unlucky trip

c) Rolf Harris is filming a new series of *Animal Hospital*

[Answer: a) a lucky trip. Although it would be unlucky for the cat if it suffered from seasickness.]

It's estimated that only 5 to 10 per cent of the world's information has been digitised.

A Scottish taxi driver earned £12,000 driving a woman with a fear of flying 16,000 miles around America.

Austria was the first country to ever use postcards.

UK fish and chip shops currently use **60,000** tonnes of fish and 500,000 tonnes of potatoes a year . . .

. . . and we eat around 300 million servings of fish and chips a year – five for every person.

The role of Hamlet is the largest part in any Shakespeare play with 1,422 lines.

There are no female speaking parts in the whole of the film *Lawrence of Arabia*.

Movie factoid, courtesy of Jonathan Ross – *Gone with the Wind* is the only Civil War epic ever filmed without a single battle scene.

California has issued six drivers licenses to people named "Jesus Christ".

Charles Dickens mentions a fried fish shop in his novel *Oliver Twist* – but it was not until the 1860s that the trade took off.
So Dickens invented them!

The world's first mobile phone was invented by Martin Cooper in April 1973.

In China, fish and chips are served with:

    a) sugar

    b) soy sauce

    c) a smile

[Answer: a) sugar. Obviously makes for some sweet 'sole' food . . .]

You share your birthday with at least 9 million other people around the world.

"**Beanz Meanz Heinz**" was voted the world's most popular advertising slogan ever. *My favourite was for milk in the 70s: "Watch out, watch out – there's a Humphrey about!"*

The first man to orbit the Earth, Yuri Gagarin, was in space for 108 minutes.

Notre Dame Cathedral was started in 1015 and completed in 1439 ... *possibly the same firm of contractors who look after the escalators on the Northern line today.*

The poet William Wordsworth could only sleep standing up.

An inventor in Brazil claims he has built a car that can run on **urine**, and does 20 miles to the gallon.
Taking the piss.

The world's largest meat pie was shared by 50,000 people at Denby Dale in Yorkshire in 2000.

Working parents with two children at school spend up to **£2,400** on childcare and entertainment during the summer holidays.

Oliver Cromwell, Lord Protector, was famed for his sense of humour and as a young man would put sticky sweets onto his guests' chairs and trick them into sitting down.

In October 1833, 10-year-old Barney Flaherty became the world's first paperboy after seeing an advert in the *New York Sun*.

In one year in New York, more than 8,000 people had been treated for dog bites – and one person suffered a penguin bite.

37

Cinderella is officially the nation's **favourite** fairy tale, followed by Sleeping Beauty and Hansel and Gretel.

Hollywood film star Fatty Arbuckle was cleared of a charge of murder, but the case ended his career.

The first known contraceptive was crocodile dung, used by Egyptians in 2000 BC.

Antarctica is the only continent without reptiles or snakes.

Washing a **chicken** before cooking it is more dangerous than not doing so. The cooking will kill any food poisoning bacteria, while washing the bird can spread bacteria to nearby taps, and kitchen surfaces.

Wayne Rooney became the youngest footballer ever to score for England when he got the first goal against Macedonia in September 2003 at the age of 17 years 317 days.

Tin Henman's great grandmother, Ellen Mary Sewell, was the first woman to serve overarm at Wimbledon ... *when he plays her now, she still beats him.*

When the UK adopted the Gregorian calendar in 1752, 11 days disappeared.

Honey is the only **food** that does not spoil.

Ivan Sergeyevich Turgenev, a Russian dramatist who died in 1883, possessed the heaviest human brain on record at nearly 4lb 7oz.

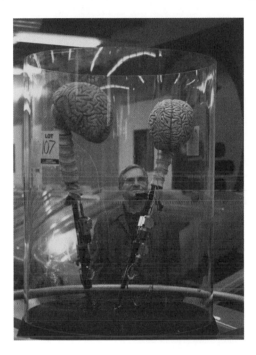

What do Chrissie Hynde, Roger Moore, Roseanne and Eddie 'The Eagle' Edwards have in common?

a) They all auditioned for the role of James Bond.

b) They all guest-presented BBC's *Top of the Pops*.

c) They all once washed dishes for a living.

[Answer: c) They all once washed dishes for a living. *Maybe one or two of them shouldn't have given up the day job.*]

The fortune cookie was invented in 1916 by George Jung, a Los Angeles noodlemaker.
(Yesterday when I was Jung.)

Scallops are considered to be the safest shellfish to eat raw.

An apple, onion and potato all have the same taste. The differences in flavour are caused by their smell. To prove this – pinch your nose and take a bite from each. They will all taste sweet.

In South Africa, termites are often roasted and eaten by the handful, like pretzels or popcorn. *Do consult with a medic if you're planning such a feast.*

Table salt is the only commodity that hasn't risen dramatically in price in the last 150 years.

In medieval England beer was often served with breakfast. *Bacon and mead please love, with all the trimmings.*

In Scotland, seeing a live haggis is supposed to be a sign of imminent good fortune. Earl Nyaff of Uirsgeul reputedly encountered one on his way to Ayr Races in 1817 and subsequently won £50.
And remember, you cannae whack a haggis.

The Chinese used to open shrimp by flaying (good word – write that down) the shells with bamboo poles. Until a few years ago, in factories where dried shrimp were being prepared, "shrimp dancers" were hired to tramp on the shells with special shoes.

Look for BBC1's exciting new series in 2007,
"Strictly Shrimp Dancing".

The letters VVSOP on a cognac bottle stand for – Very Very Superior Old Pale.

Grapes explode when you put them in the microwave.

Cranberries are sorted for ripeness by bouncing them up and down; a fully ripened cranberry can be **dribbled** like a basketball.

Before it was unsolicited email, **spam** was of course a luncheon meat. It is so resistant to spoilage that, if kept in the closed can, it may well outlast eternity and will certainly live longer than you. *Spam, spam, lovely spam!*

Wine will **spoil** if exposed to light, hence tinted bottles.
P.S. No one says hence any more.

Contrary to popular belief, the number **57** on Heinz products does not represent the number of varieties of pickles the company once had; it was actually chosen by Henry Heinz because of the 'special' significance of the numbers '5' and '7'.

It has many more now, including the delicious 'Big Soup', and the stupendous curried beans.

Fanta Orange is the **third** largest selling soft drink in the world.

Alcoholic lemonade is outselling **premium** bottled lagers in British pubs.

Over a third of all pineapples come from **Hawaii**.

A turkey should never be carved until it has been out of the oven at least 30 minutes. This allows the inner cooking to subside and the internal meat juices to stop running. Once the meat sets, it's easier to carve clean, neat slices.

There are more than **15,000** different kinds of rice.

Beer foam will go down by **licking** your finger then sticking it in the beer. *Do get permission from a hygienist first.*

Ancient Greeks and Romans believed asparagus had medicinal qualities for helping prevent bee stings and relieve **toothaches**.

Worcestershire Sauce is **basically** anchovy ketchup.
Put like that ...

During the Middle Ages, almost all beef, pork, mutton and chicken was chopped finely. **Forks** were unknown at the time and the knife was a kitchen utensil rather than a piece of tableware.

For TV beer commercials, they add **liquid** detergent to the beer to make it foam more.

Milk delivered to shops today was in the cow two days ago.

Brussels sprouts are called Brussels sprouts because they were discovered in Brussels. *So now you know.*

Flamingo tongues were a common delicacy at Roman feasts. *It was a unique food that could stand on one leg.*

The wheat that produces a one-pound loaf of bread requires 2 tons of water to grow.

There are 2,000,000 different combinations of sandwiches that can be created from a SUBWAY menu.

Most common sports drinks are the equivalent of sugar-sweetened human sweat. That is, they have the same salt concentration as sweat.

Ketchup was sold in the 1830s as:

a) Hair tonic

b) Furniture polish

c) Medicine

[Answer: c) Medicine. Not so incredible really: it still manages to cure reluctant appetites among the younger diners.]

Scientists have recently discovered that the humble lettuce was an ancient form of Viagra, which could boost your sexual performance. In small amounts, it has a sedative effect, but in larger doses acts like a sexual stimulant. *Surely everyone's lost interest after you've spent 50 minutes eating a lettuce ...*

Dunkin' Donuts serves about **112,500** doughnuts each day.

Now, the story of chopsticks. Well, the Chinese developed the custom of using chopsticks because they didn't need anything resembling a knife and fork at the table. They cut up food into bite-sized pieces in the kitchen before serving it. This stemmed from their belief that bringing meat to the table in any form resembling an animal was uncivilized and that it was, in any case, inhospitable to ask a guest to cut food while eating.

Europeans drink more wine than Americans. France and Italy produce over 40% of all wine consumed in the world.

There are more than 7,000 varieties of apples grown in the world. The apples from one tree can fill 20 boxes every year. Each box weighs an average of 42 pounds.

Bananas contain a natural chemical which can make a person happy. This same chemical is found in Prozac.

Carrots were first grown as a medicine not a food. The Ancient Greeks called carrots "Karoto". *Modern Greeks do, too!*

In Australia, the Number 1 topping for pizza is eggs. In Chile, the favourite topping is mussels and clams. In the United States, it's pepperoni. *And in Britain, it's Kit Kat. No, really it's cheese and tomato.*

It takes more than **500** peanuts to make one 12-ounce jar of peanut butter.

Sausages are called **bangers** because during World War Two they contained so much water they exploded when fried.

The National Sausage and **Hot Dog Council** says when children were asked what they would like on their hot dogs if their mums weren't watching, 25 per cent said they would prefer chocolate sauce.

The dark meat on a roast turkey has more calories than the white meat. *So eat it all up, I don't want to see anything left on that plate.*

Ovaltine, the drink made of milk, malt, egg and cocoa, was developed in 1904 in Berne, Switzerland. It was originally named Ovomaltine. A clerical error changed it when the manufacturer registered the name.

Sixty cows can produce a ton of milk a day.

The great silent movie star Charlie Chaplin had his **feet** insured for £33,497.

Fire-fighters returned to their station in Dallas after a fire to find it ablaze. *Potatoes* had been left cooking on a stove.

The first full-length episode of *The Simpsons* **was screened in December 1989 and was entitled** "Simpsons Roasting on an Open Fire".

No two zebras have the same pattern of stripes.

Friday **13** th

Any month that starts on a Sunday will have a Friday the 13th **in it.**

Richard the Lionheart only visited England **twice** during his reign and could only speak French.

Actor and director Gene Wilder's screen debut was as an undertaker in *Bonnie and Clyde*.

If the sun stopped shining, it would take us **eight** minutes to be aware of it. *Okay, who worked that out and how?*

The first single to top the charts posthumously was "(Sittin' on) the Dock of the Bay" by Otis Redding.

British actor Colin Firth became an Arsenal fan after filming *Fever Pitch* in which he played the part of . . . an Arsenal fan.

Swing singer and crooner Harry Connick Jnr started playing the piano at the age of three.

Aircraft are forbidden to fly over the Taj Mahal.

The first TV to be installed in a house was in Harrow in 1926.

The **blood** in the shower scene in *Psycho* was actually chocolate syrup.

About 1.6 million British women have hair-loss problems.

If you counted every star in the galaxy at a rate of one every second, it would take you 3,000 years to count them all.

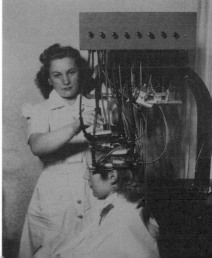

It's estimated that by the year 2021 the morning rush hour will start at 5am.

England football international Sol Campbell's first name is actually Sulzeer.

40% of the world's newspapers are printed on paper from Canada's forests.

Alexander the Great died of alcoholism at the age of 32.

The seven modern Wonders of the World are: the Colosseum of Rome; the Catacombs of Alexandria; the Great Wall of China; Stonehenge; the Leaning Tower of Pisa; the Porcelain Tower of Nanking, *and Keanu Reeves' acting.*

The director of the US Patent Office **resigned** in 1875 because he claimed there was nothing left to invent.

Eugene Shoemaker fulfilled his dream of going to the moon – but only when he was dead. **His ashes were taken aboard a rocket from Cape Canaveral.**

The most popular pub name in Britain is the Red Lion. *No red lion was harmed in the making of this factoid.*

A fully grown oak tree expels **seven tons** of water through its leaves in a day.

The film rights of the play *The Mousetrap*, which opened in 1957, were sold on condition the film would only be released after the play closed . . .

A parking space in a Cornish town sold for £15,000 because spaces are so hard to come by.

Medical experts have noticed that people who stutter rarely do so when alone or when talking to pets.

Mouth ulcers are caused by brushing your teeth too vigorously, biting your mouth, burning it with hot food or drink, or stress.

The first ever *Top of the Pops* was broadcast in 1964 and the presenter was Jimmy Savile.

Alf Garnett actor Warren Mitchell was once a disc jockey on Radio Luxembourg under his real name, Warren Misel.
– Warren Misel in the evening.

When The Beatles failed an audition with Decca Records in 1962, the label chose Brian Poole and the Tremeloes instead.

Villagers in Great Henney, Essex, built a decoy spire on their 11th century church to prevent amorous woodpeckers from causing damage to the original spire.

If you visit someone on the Isle of Man on January 1st and don't bring a gift with you it's bad luck and will mean a bad year to come.

The average slug can stretch itself out to 11 times its body length ... *How generous. Gee, they spoil us, those slugs.*

Ewan McGregor's mum Carole has a cameo role in his film
Shallow Grave **as a prospective flatmate.**

The first female to run for Vice President in the USA was
Geraldine Ferraro, as Walter Mondale's running mate in 1984.

At one point there was a **five-year** waiting list to be in
the audience for a recording of TV show, *Bullseye*.

The highest ever winning score in *University Challenge* was
520 by University College, Oxford, in 1987.

**The mascots for BBC2 when it was launched on 20 April 1964
were Hullabaloo and Custard, two kangaroos.**

The king of hearts is the only king without a **moustache**
in a standard pack of playing cards.

**Composer Frederic Chopin
slept with wooden wedges
between his fingers as a
child to extend their span.**

FIRE RET

SEC

The substance known as
Plaster of Paris . . .

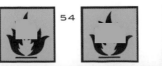

ARDANT
TION

. . . is fire retardant.

Football historians voted the Brazilian, Pele, as the greatest **footballer** of the 20th century.

Actor Yul Brynner made an advert which was shown on TV after his death in which he said: "Hello, I'm dead; smoking killed me."

Instead of hitting snooze when the alarm goes, take ten deep breaths, which will make you more alert by getting energising oxygen into your lungs.

Robbie Williams' "**Angels**" is the most requested funeral song. Sinatra's "**My Way**" is next.

Maggie Thatcher Day is celebrated on January 10 in the Falkland Islands.

Red Vineyard was the only painting Van Gogh sold during his lifetime. *What's that you say?*

Canadian teenager Mike Rowe
had to give up his website
mikerowesoft.com
when he got a letter from
Microsoft lawyers.

The most number of enrolled students in Britain are with the Open University.

Lincoln Cathedral had the highest spire in Britain, at 524ft, until it was blown down in 1584.

Not only did *Forrest Gump* win an Oscar for Best Film in 1995 but its star Tom Hanks won the Best Actor award and Robert Zemeckis won Best Director.

It's a factoid that laughing can burn off six calories a minute.

Santa's red coat is a relatively new introduction. Most images of Father Christmas prior to about 1880 showed him with a green coat. Red became the most popular colour after its US introduction by Coca-Cola during the 1930s.

Cockroaches have a high tolerance to radiation and are the most likely creature to survive a nuclear war. *Whoever said life was fair?*

Vivien Leigh beat 1,399 rivals to the part of Scarlett in *Gone with the Wind*.

Watching football can cause injuries. Not from fights, but "cheering-related" injuries such as shoulder complaints and sprained necks from leaping out of seats when a goal is scored.

Marvin Gaye's song "Let's Get It On" is top of the love-making charts for couples planning a night of **passion**.

The only underground station in London to be named after a football club is called Arsenal. Travellers used to get off at Gillespie Road.

The Angel of the North near Gateshead is the largest sculpture of an angel in the world.

Horseradish is a member of the cabbage family.

Cherophobia is a fear of **fun**.

The largest iceberg ever was spotted adrift in the Atlantic. It was bigger than Wales.

Yuri Gagarin, the first man into space, is buried in the Kremlin wall.

An English breakfast is the thing most ex-pats miss most. English cheese, marmalade and Marmite are also on the list . . . *Must be a sticky list then.*

Charlotte, Emily and Anne – the Brontë sisters – all died of tuberculosis and were all outlived by their father.

A group of bullfinches is known as a bellowing.

Hard man Geordie actor Jimmy Nail wore a ballet dress, a mackintosh and pit boots when he once sang in the band King Crabs.

Four out of five computer **passwords** are chosen from sporting heroes, pets or family members.

Cheesemakers added lemon to their cheese when the Duke of Edinburgh visited. It made the cheese inedible but the factory smell nice.

Mother's Day is the third largest card-sending holiday.

The longest bone in the human body is the femur.
As you can see here ...

The first Queen Elizabeth destroyed all the mirrors in her palace when she got **old** so she couldn't see her reflection. *She did have 140 years of bad luck though. Always wondered why.*

Dr Alex Comfort's *The Joy of Sex* **has been translated into 24 languages.**

George I was nicknamed the **Turnip-Hoer** after suggesting that St James' Park be turned into a turnip field.

Leaving the house without any **underwear** on is a crime in Thailand. *How do they know?*

Louis Armstrong is the oldest artiste to have a No 1 single – "What a Wonderful World" – when he was **67**. The song has been used in 18 British TV commercials.

Fleas can jump 80 times their own height and 150 times their own length.

The Black Death, in the 14th century, is reckoned to be the world's worst epidemic, with an estimated 75 million deaths.

The **smallest** country in the world is Vatican City, which measures just 0.44sq km.

Armadillos give birth to quadruplets of the same sex.
And sweet Marie, who waits for me.

Ithyphallophobia is a morbid fear of seeing, thinking about or having an erect penis ... *Never had that one.*

A man in Florida sued a topless club because a dancer with a 60-inch bust thrust her breasts into his face with such ferocity he claimed he had suffered **whiplash** injuries.

In the Aztec culture **avocados** were considered so sexually powerful that virgins were restricted from contact with them.

The average shelf-life of a latex condom is about two years.

According to a survey of sex shop owners, cherry is the most popular flavour of **edible** underwear. Chocolate is the least popular. *Cabbage was the last one mentioned in the survey.*

Marilyn Monroe, the most celebrated sex icon of the 20th century, confessed to a friend that despite her three husbands and a parade of lovers, she had never had an orgasm.

"Venus observa" is the technical term for the "**missionary position**".

A two-ton **rhino** tried to hump a car at a safari park. It dented the doors and ripped off the wing mirrors. The driver eventually managed to drive off, with the rhino in pursuit.
And the elephant never forgets …

Formicophilia is the fetish for having ants or small insects crawl on your genitals. *That's not a terribly common fetish as far as I know. A new Bushtucker Trial perhaps?*

A man's beard grows fastest when he anticipates sex.

The female bedbug has no sexual opening. To get around this dilemma, the male uses his curved penis to drill a vagina into the female.
Well, they might be lazy those bedbugs, but they're not thick.

Masturbation **was once believed to lead to blindness, madness, sudden death and other unpleasant diseases.** *Present research, however, shows no connection.*

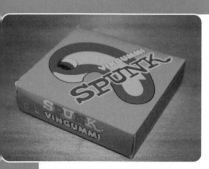

A man will ejaculate
approximately 18 quarts
of **semen**, containing
half a trillion sperm.
*Not all at once – in his
lifetime.*

A medical study showed that people who have **sex**
once or twice a week have their immune systems
boosted slightly.

**The first couple to be shown in bed together on prime
time television were Fred and Wilma Flintstone.**

The **kiss** that is given by the bride to the groom at the
end of the wedding ceremony originates from the
earliest times when the couple would actually make
love for the first time under the eyes of half the village!
What's that all about?

In Alexandria, Minnesota, it's **illegal** for a
husband to have sex with his wife if his breath
smells of garlic, onions, sardines . . . *or spam.*

The more sex you have, the more you will be offered. The sexually active body gives off greater quantities of chemicals called **pheromones**.

The earliest known illustration of a man using a **condom** during sexual intercourse is painted on the wall of a cave in France. It is dated between 12,000 and 15,000 years old.

When women make love they produce amounts of the *hormone* oestrogen, which makes hair shine and skin smooth.

A lot of lovemaking can **unblock** a stuffy nose. Sex is a natural antihistamine. It can help combat asthma and hay fever.

Kissing each day will keep the dentist away. Kissing encourages saliva to wash food from the teeth and lowers the level of the acid that causes decay, preventing plaque build-up.

According to a U.S. market research firm, the most popular American **bra** size is currently 36C, up from 1991 when it was 34B.

On the net, for every "normal" webpage, there are **five** porn pages.

Sex is an instant cure for mild depression. It releases **endorphins** into the bloodstream, producing a sense of euphoria and leaving you with a feeling of well-being.

Male bats have the highest rate of **homosexuality** of any mammal.

Humans are the only animals that **copulate** face to face.

32% of women in Russia have never had an **orgasm**. *Who does that research?*

When a woman first has **sex** with her husband, her mum must be in the room to witness the act, in Colombia.

According to psychologists, the shoe and the foot are the most common sources of sexual *fetishism* in Western society.

Gentle, relaxed **lovemaking** reduces your chances of suffering dermatitis, skin rashes and blemishes. The sweat produced cleanses the pores and makes your skin glow.

There are approximately 100 million acts of sexual **intercourse** performed each day.

During World War Two, **condoms** were used to cover rifle barrels to prevent them from being damaged by salt water as the soldiers swam to shore.

According to legislation in Kentucky, 'No **female** shall appear in a bathing suit on the highway unless escorted by two police officers.' *The police force is the most popular profession in Kentucky – the cops say it's finger-lickin' good.*

Sex is biochemically no different from eating large quantities of **chocolate**.

Research shows that professors who smoke are twice as likely to write a book as those who do not.

The **largest** island in the Mediterranean Sea is Sicily.

The world's three best-selling newspapers are all published in Russian.

The first letters of the months July through November, in order, spell the name JASON.

The first American flags were made of hemp cloth.

At the beginning of the 18th century only half of the population ever ate meat.

The average person presses the snooze button on their alarm clock **three** times each morning.

The average web page contains 500 words.

The cashew **nut** belongs to the poison ivy family.
Who is Poison Ivy?
A friend of Aloe Vera?

Superstition says that the left side is the wrong side of the bed.

The average adult can **read** 150–200 words a minute.

The UK flag is called the Union Flag – it is called the Union Jack when it's flown from the jack mast of a ship.

During one period of extreme political instability in **Mexico**, three men were president in one day.

EastEnders mutt **Wellard** – acting dog and full Equity member – appeared in the Russell Crowe blockbuster *Gladiator*.

Tony Robinson only got the part of Baldrick in the *Blackadder* series after Timothy Spall turned it down.

Jack Nicholson's art collection is worth more than $150 million.

Racing driver **Jenson Button** failed his driving test first time around. According to the terrified examiner, he nipped in between two cars "through a gap that wasn't there".

In the mid-90s, a photo of *Desperate Housewives* star **Teri Hatcher**, wrapped in nothing but a red Superman cape, became the most downloaded image on America Online.

Ronan Keating was the most imitated singer during the final round of auditions for the recent series of *Stars in their Eyes*.

Nicolas Cage was born Nicolas Coppola but changed his name to distance himself from his uncle, the famous director Francis Ford Coppola. He chose Cage from the comic book character, Luke Cage.

Spoon bender Uri Geller stands on his head once a day. *Takes all sorts.*

Rolf Harris was the Australian Junior Backstroke champion in 1946.

Jude Law's real first name is the not so cool David. Jude is his middle name. *Well, so says his mum, L.A.*

Sir Paul McCartney can't read or write music.

Between 1968 and 1976 **Harrison Ford** had only three acting jobs. *This isn't one of them.*

Charlie Chaplin has been portrayed on screen by more actors than anyone else.

In the early episodes of *Star Trek*, **Dr McCoy**'s medical scanner was actually a normal salt shaker.

Halle Berry is diabetic.

When *Doctor Who* first began, each episode was made on a budget of just £2,500.

Doctor Who's **TARDIS** is a Type 40.

Claire Sweeney once lost a stone and a half in weight so she would look good in a wedding dress for a scene in *Brookside*.

Jada Pinkett-Smith was turned down for the part of Will Smith's girlfriend in *The Fresh Prince of Bel-Air* because the producers thought she looked too short next to him. They married on New Year's Eve in 1997.
That's Jada and Will, not the producers.

At the age of 11 **Pierce Brosnan** was almost six feet tall, but he was still the target of bullies due to his being Irish.

Jamie Theakston has one of the most popular noses amongst men who have nose jobs.

When supermodel **Claudia Schiffer** starred in a lingerie advertising campaign for retailer H&M in 2000, residents in her native Germany stole hundreds of the posters from billboards around the country.

Justin Hawkins from **The Darkness** once composed and performed a jingle for an IKEA commercial.

Tom Baker was not first choice to play the fourth Doctor Who. **Graham Crowden**, who went on to appear in the sitcom *Waiting for God*, was initially offered the role but turned it down as he didn't want to tie himself to one part. **Michael Bentine**, **Jim Dale** and **Fulton Mackay** were also considered before Baker was cast.

Simon Cowell
once appeared on *Top of the Pops* dressed up as a dog.

36 cameras follow the housemates' every move in *Big Brother*.

Christina Aguilera
has a vocal range of four octaves.

In the early 1980s **Ricky Gervais** was part of a New Romantic synthesizer group called Seona Dancing. The band reached number 116 and 70 in the charts with their first two releases before being dropped by their record company.

Sean Wilson was finally cast as Martin Platt in *Coronation Street* after having previously been rejected for the roles of both Terry Duckworth and Kevin Webster.

The day Naked Chef **Jamie Oliver** was spotted by television producers working at the River Café, he had only come into work because another chef was ill.

In 1999, **Hilary Swank** became the second actress to win an Oscar for playing a member of the opposite sex in *Boys Don't Cry*. The first was Linda Hunt, who played a man opposite **Mel Gibson** in 1983 film *The Year of Living Dangerously*.

Star Trek was originally going to be called 'Wagon Train to the Stars'.

EastEnders' **Dennis Rickman, actor Nigel Harman**, made his first television appearance at the age of eight, in a stock cube commercial.

Stephen Fry claims to hold the British record for uttering the most profanities on television during one live broadcast. *Shush, Stephen – don't tell Gordon Ramsay – he'll be very jealous ...*

Supermodel **Gisele Bündchen** earned £50,000 in less than an hour for modelling just three bikinis at a Brazilian fashion show in 2001.

Harry Potter author JK Rowling wrote her first story – "Rabbit" – when she was just five years old.

Super supermodel **Claudia Schiffer** pays £120 every fortnight for a car wash.

Despite being used to front a long-running advertising campaign for John Smith's bitter, **Jack Dee** is teetotal.

After **Cliff Richard** appeared on the ITV music show *Oh Boy!* in 1958, newspapers attacked him for his "crude exhibitionism". One even warned parents:

"Don't let your daughter go out with people like this."

Jeremy Paxman, host of *University Challenge*, was turned down as a contestant for the show during his student days.

David and **Victoria Beckham** were so impressed with **Ronni Ancona** and **Alistair McGowan**'s impersonations of them that the Beckhams tried to hire them for a party. The impressionists declined.

Santa Claus has a **brother** named Bells Nichols, according to French tradition.

The mythical Scottish town of Brigadoon appears for one day every 100 years.

Nobody laid claim to the Nobel Peace Prize in 1972. *So if you think you know who won the Nobel Peace Prize in 1972, do let the United Nations know.*

If we had the same mortality rate as in the 1900s, over half the people in the world would not be alive.

Paranormal experts say people reach the peak of their ability to see ghosts when they are seven years old.

One year is exactly 365 days, five hours, 48 minutes and 54.5 seconds.

The launching mechanism of an aircraft carrier, which helps planes take off, could throw a pickup truck over a **mile**.

The largest known prime number is *7,816,230* digits long.

The elephant is the only animal with four knees.

The only naturally **blue** food is the Irish Bilberry.

A bolt of lighting can strike the earth with a force as great as 100,000,000 volts.

A rainbow can only occur when the sun is 40 degrees or less above the horizon.

A Boeing 747's wingspan is longer than the Wright brothers' first flight.
I know, I was there with my brother, Laurence.

One year contains 31,557,600 seconds.

50,000 of the cells in your body will die and be replaced with new cells while you read this factoid.

Astronaut **Neil Armstrong** stepped on the moon with his left foot first. *When Neil Armstrong arrived to be interviewed on my radio programme in the 8os, he was brought over to the UK by a PR company who were promoting a well-known shaver. As we're about to open the microphone and invite Neil into the studio, a PR lady pops her head round the door and says: "Steve – Neil's in the green room and he's all ready for the interview. Just one thing though – no questions about the Moon."*

Impotence is legal grounds for divorce in **24** American states.

7 per cent of Americans eat McDonald's each day. *They're quite easy to spot.*

An albatross can fly all day and **not** flap its wings once.

A chameleon's tongue is twice the length of its body. *Even longer if it's a stand-up chameleon.*

Film director Alfred Hitchcock never won an Academy Award for directing.

The earth weighs about 6,588,000,000,000 million tons.

Australia is the richest source of mineral sands in the world.

The opposite sides of a die **always** add up to seven.

A coat hanger is forty-four inches long if straightened.
And a handy radio aerial.

Live Aid/Live 8 section

In July **1985**, the original Live Aid boasted 100 artists, a million spectators and 2 billion viewers.

"Do They Know it's Christmas" was the fastest-selling single ever . . . **Bob Geldof** had expected the song to raise £70,000. Astoundingly, it raised £8 million.

The Live Aid concert coined in more than £40 million for famine relief.

Prince Charles and **Princess Diana** were in the crowd at Wembley Stadium.

Phil Collins started the day performing solo in Wembley before singing two duets with **Sting**. He then flew on Concorde to New York, where a helicopter took him to Philadelphia. He played drums for **Eric Clapton**, before repeating the same songs he had played in London.

The glorious summer sunshine ensured that temperatures soared to over **90 degrees** inside Wembley, with concertgoers at the front needing to be hosed down by security staff.

Bob Geldof became so excited when performing with The Boomtown Rats that he pulled his microphone out of its socket.

The Who's performance at Live Aid was literally explosive: halfway through their set the amplifier blew up, so only the stadium's audience heard their renditions of "Pinball Wizard" and "My Generation".

In 2005, 20 years after the original Live Aid, rock stars from all over the world were once again persuaded by **Bob Geldof** and **Bono** of **U2** to play a series of gigs across the planet called Live 8, to coincide with the G8 Summit. *Here now, some factoids from the day ...*

Portsmouth was chosen as one of the cities to show the London Live 8 concert on a big screen, but the local council turned down the chance because the event clashed with the International Festival of the Sea. Chancellor Gordon Brown waived bills for staging the Live 8 concerts in a move equivalent to writing off £500,000 in VAT.

Prince Charles' charity The Prince's Trust cancelled its annual Party in the Park concert in London, to make way for Live 8. The Prince of Wales' charity was given £1.6 million from the Live 8 concert for the privilege.

85% of the world's population were able to tune into to the Live 8 concerts through a variety of media. They were broadcast in more than **140 countries**, on TV, radio, online and even through mobile phones.

The Live 8 concerts were the largest worldwide TV broadcast in history, according to organisers.

Among the artists performing worldwide at Live 8 was **Dido** – who was the **Phil Collins** of the new millennium – she performed at three Live 8 concerts in one day – London, Cornwall and Paris.

Live Aid/Live 8 section

The UK's National Health Service is the **third** largest employer in the world, after the Red Army in China and the Indian railway.

The little circle of paper that is cut out after a paper has been punched by a hole-puncher is called a "**chad**".

The *only* English place that has a name that ends with an exclamation mark is Westward Ho!.

A cactus in Phoenix, Arizona, **killed** a man. David Grundman fired two shotgun blasts at a giant saguaro cactus that ended up falling on top of him.

In China, September 20 is "Love Your Teeth Day".

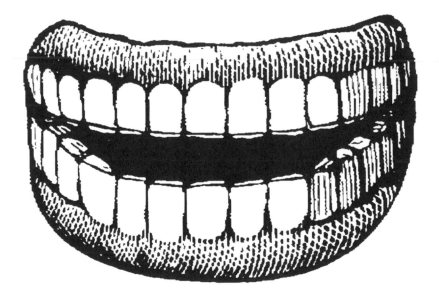

English sailors were referred to as "limeys" because sailors added lime juice to their diet to combat scurvy.

The name "Muppet" was coined by Jim Henson. The word was made from a combination of the word "marionette" and "puppet". *Jim Henson was sent a stustificut of congratulations, signed by the Old Woman.*

A Japanese artist, Tadahiko Ogawa, made a copy of the *Mona Lisa* completely out of **toast**.

A blink lasts approximately 0.3 seconds.

Smokers are likely to **die** on average six and a half years earlier than non-smokers.

Actor Adrien Brody **sold** his car and flat in preparation for filming for *The Pianist* so he could identify with the dispossessed character he played. It worked, as he won an Oscar for his performance.

Food can only be tasted if it is mixed with saliva.

Twenty per cent more heart attacks occur on Monday mornings because of the stress of going back to work after the weekend.

The **space** between your eyebrows is called the glabella. *Aah, you can't have everything Liam Gallagher.*

The first example of a television soap opera was *The Appleyards*, which ran from 1952 to 1957. It was shown fortnightly and was aimed at children.

The term "**soap opera**" derives from American radio in the 1930s when soap and detergent companies such as Proctor and Gamble sponsored programmes.

During the 16th century, newly married couples in France had to stand **naked** outdoors while the groom kissed the bride's left foot and big toe as part of traditional customs.

More people are alive **today**, than have ever died.

The town of Bunol, near Valencia, Spain has a festival called **"Tomatina"** on the last Wednesday in August. People throw hundreds of tomatoes at each other, and the festival is considered the world's largest food fight.

Alexander the Great made his troops eat **onions** as he believed it would improve their vitality.

Before football referees started using whistles in 1878, they used to rely on waving a **handkerchief**.

In ancient Egypt, priests plucked every hair from their bodies including their eyebrows and eyelashes.

There are 13,000 different varieties of roses in the world.

If you superimpose Leonardo Da Vinci's face over that of the *Mona Lisa*, you will find that the bone structures are identical.

There are approximately 35,000 Elvis impersonators world-wide.

The lower section of the average person's arm – between the elbow and the wrist – is exactly the same length as their **feet**.

In one year the human heart pumps approximately **1,600,000** gallons of blood through the human body.

The **Empire State Building** in New York City is constructed of more than **10** million bricks.

Workers at a Las Vegas hospital were suspended for placing bets on when patients would die.

The electric chair was invented by a **dentist**.

The number of marriages in England and Wales increased in the last year for the second year in a row. Grooms are 31.2 years old on average and brides 28.9, according to the Office of National Statistics.

"Underground" is the only word in the English language that begins and ends with the letters "und".

During the average human life, you will eat 70 assorted bugs, as well as 10 spiders, whilst you sleep. *Bet you've often wondered why it's not every day you wake up hungry...*

Whenever people accidentally trip over themselves whilst walking, they automatically go into "**survival mode**" and try to pretend that they meant it, e.g. they start into a jog.

The Statue of Liberty's nose is 4ft 6in long.
That's actually bigger than mine!

Cockney rhyming slang for soap is "Cape of Good Hope".

The term "**mayday**" used for signalling for help comes from the French "M'aidez", which means "Help me".

If you keep your eyes **open** by force during a sneeze, they can pop out.

51 per cent of Italian women between the ages of 20 and 60 believe that cheating on spouses is healthy for a relationship.

The name Wendy was created for the book *Peter Pan*. There was **no** recorded "Wendy" prior to that.

WEE SE

You can see
how hydrated
you are by
checking the colour
of your urine.

CTION

If it's a dark yellow
to yellowish-green,
you are under-hydrated.
If it's light yellow
to clear, you're very
well hydrated.

In 1845, President Andrew Jackson's pet parrot was removed from his funeral for swearing.

The first golf ball to be hit on the **Moon** was by Alan Shepard on February 6, 1971.

Poland's Stella Walsh (Stanislawa Walasiewicz) won the women's 100 metre race at the 1932 Olympics in Los Angeles. When she was killed in 1980 as an innocent victim in a robbery attempt, an autopsy declared her to be a male.

The average person falls asleep in seven minutes.

A human **head** remains conscious for about 15 to 20 seconds after it has been decapitated.

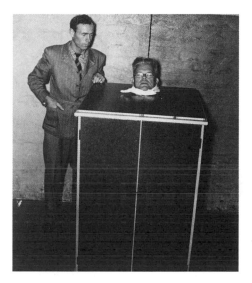

The world's first rollercoaster opened in 1884 at Coney Island, New York. It was designed by Lemarcus Thompson, a former Sunday school teacher.

The Mousetrap by Agatha Christie is the **longest** running play in history.

Ancient Egyptians shaved **off their eyebrows to mourn the death of their cats.** *Why? The cats don't care – they're raving dead!*

John Milton used **8,000** different words in his poem, *Paradise Lost.*

All of the roles in Shakespeare's plays were originally acted by men and boys. In England at that time, it wasn't **proper** for females to appear on stage.

> **All time classic factoid: barbers at one time combined shaving and haircutting with bloodletting and pulling teeth. The white stripes on a field of red that spiral down a barber pole represent the bandages used in the bloodletting.**

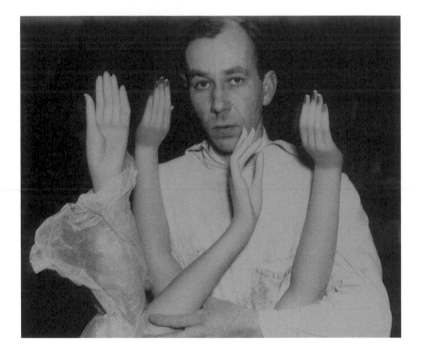

Women shoplift more often than men; the statistics are 4 to 1.
My brother was once a maniokleptic – he used to put stuff back.

Q: How many American presidents are not buried in the United States? **A**: Five: Gerald Ford, Jimmy Carter, George Bush, Bill Clinton and George W Bush. *Caught you out, see?!*

The average person walks the equivalent of twice around the world in their lifetime.

A person afflicted with hexadectylism has six fingers or six toes on one or both hands and feet. *Obviously makes buying gloves a unique experience.*

Julius Caesar, Martin Luther and Jonathan Swift all suffered from **Ménière's disease**. It is a disorder of the ear causing problems with balance and hissing, roaring or whistling sounds to be perceived.

The average male will spend 2,965 hours shaving during his lifetime.

When offered a new pen to write with, 97% of all people will write their own name.

The vocabulary of the average person consists of **5,000** to **6,000** words. *Unless you're a guest on the Trisha Show, in which case it's less than 20. No offence.*

Dr Seuss wrote *Green Eggs and Ham* after his editor dared him to write a book using fewer than 50 different words.

The Eiffel Tower in Paris has 2,500,000 rivets in it.

All the proceeds earned from James M. Barrie's book *Peter Pan* were bequeathed to the Great Ormond Street Hospital for the Sick Children in London.

Alfred Hitchcock didn't have a belly button. It was eliminated when he was sewn up after surgery. *(Perhaps that's too much information.)*

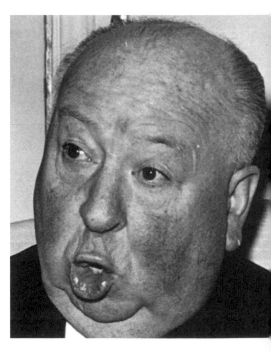

Singapore has only one train station.

You are more likely to be killed by a champagne cork
than by a poisonous **spider**.

A group of **frogs** is called an army.

A group of **rhinos** is called a crash.

A group of **kangaroos** is called a mob.

A group of **crows** is called a murder.

A group of **officers** is called a mess.

A group of **larks** is called an exaltation.

A group of **vultures** is called a wake.

And that group of **factoids** is called a factcluster.

The **starfish** is the only animal that can turn its stomach
inside out. *Unless you include Matt Lucas.*

The milk of a **hippo** is bright pink.

**When a giraffe's baby is born
it falls from a height of six feet,
normally without being hurt.**

"I ate your mum last week," said **Kerry Katona** to 60,000 cockroaches at the start of a Bushtucker trial in *I'm a Celebrity ... Get Me Out of Here!*

Royal-watcher **Jennie Bond** chewed her way through a leaf mimic, a yabby, a stick insect, a wichetty grub and a fish eye in *I'm a Celebrity ... Get Me Out of Here!*

Reality show star **Jade Goody** appeared in the first episode of *London's Burning* when she was five years old.

Some of the stars in *I'm a Celebrity ... Get Me Out of Here!* started eating their toothpaste they were so hungry, according to **Joe Pasquale**, jungle champion of Autumn 2004.

The producers of television's *I'm a Celebrity ... Get Me Out of Here!* reportedly asked **Joe Pasquale** to tone down his squeaky voice whilst out in the jungle, in case the high pitch attracted dingos.

Maria Burrell, wife of **Paul**, said she begged her husband not to go into the jungle for *I'm a Celebrity… Get Me Out of Here!* "I knew the press would have a field day," she said. *And they did.*

Now a BBC TV presenter, builder **Craig Phillips** won £70,000 in the first ever UK *Big Brother*, which launched in July 2000.

Marjorie was the name of the pet chicken in the first *Big Brother* and **Juanita** the toy baby.

UK Pop Idol won the Golden Rose of Montreaux in 2002 – a TV prize normally won by acclaimed dramas and comedy shows.

More than **one hundred million** votes were cast during the first series of *American Idol*.

Celebrity Big Brother 3 contestant, equestrian **John McCririck**, blamed his Harrow education for his attitude to women, which includes calling his wife "The Booby" after a South American bird which isn't very bright and squawks a lot.

Contestants in *Celebrity Big Brother 3* had to warm the lavatory seat for ex-DJ Lisa I'Anson when she played the role of house queen.

I'm A Celebrity ... Get Me Out of Here! star **Vic Reeves**' real name is James Moir. He adopted his pseudonym after singers Vic Damone and Jim Reeves.

X Factor presenter **Kate Thornton** was the youngest ever editor of *Smash Hits* magazine. She took over the role when she was just 23 years old.

Celebrity Big Brother star **Brigitte Nielsen** once reportedly turned down $1 million to spend a night with an Arab prince.

Will Young's "Evergreen" was the biggest-selling debut single in history, selling 385,483 copies in its first 24 hours.

Reality TV star and singer **Kerry Katona** and TV's **Chris Evans** both attended the same school.

I'm A Celebrity ... Get Me Out of Here! star **Tara Palmer-Tomkinson** once attended Debtors Anonymous after spending £50,000 on designer clothes.

Supermodel **Caprice** told housemates in *Celebrity Big Brother 3* she hated men who "flagellate". *She was talking about flatulence.*

10,000 hours of tape are recorded during any one series of *Big Brother*.

Stroking a cat or dog lowers blood pressure and heart rate and helps **reduce** the risk of illnesses like heart disease. *Not in the dog – in you.*

The **longest** recorded tapeworm in the human body was 33 metres long. It's said that in the 60s, fashion models used to eat tapeworm to stay thin. *That's not funny – that's true.*

When the Monster Raving Loony Party was founded in **1963** its manifesto included the vote at 18, local radio stations and all-day pub opening.

Film star Charlie Chaplin once won **third** place in a Charlie Chaplin lookalike contest. *But he stayed silent about it.*

A Sultan's wife is called a **Sultana**.

A turbot lays 14 million eggs during its lifetime. *What on earth is a turbot? Answers on a postcard please to Captain Birdseye.*

More Britons than ever own a second home abroad – Spain is the favourite location, followed by France. Then Jersey. *Then the Isle of Dogs.*

Uranus is the only planet that rotates on its side. *Oooo, Matron!*

The can opener wasn't invented until 48 years after the **can**. *I've still got 53,000 cans of tinned peaches to open.*

In Italy, a man can be arrested if he wears a skirt in public.

In the Dark Ages it was thought that when you sneezed, a brief opportunity for devils to enter your mouth was present, thus explains the origins of **"Bless you"**.

A novel written in **1892** by Jack McCullough, entitled *Golf In The Year 2000*, referred to digital watches, bullet trains and driverless golf carts. *That's nothing – Jack once sent me a text.*

Tuesday is the most productive day of the working week.

The Ramses brand of condoms is named after the great pharaoh Ramses II, who fathered more than 160 children.

Sounds like he never wore one himself, then.

"**Go**." is the shortest complete sentence in the English language.

The velocity of your cough can be up to 60mph, but the mighty **sneeze** can reach up to 100mph.

In the 18th century all carrots were either purple or white. *Dutch* farmers decided to plant and cultivate orange crops as it was their national colour.

The most commonly used word in English conversation is
" **I** "

The word "**queue**" is the only word in the English language that is still pronounced the same way when the last four letters are removed.

The only country in the world that has a Bill of Rights for *Cows* is India.

You use more **calories** eating celery than there are in the celery itself.

The only wood used by cabinet maker Thomas Chippendale was **mahogany**.

Mercury is the only metal that is **liquid** at room temperature.

Libra, the Scales, is the only inanimate symbol in the zodiac.

The only part of the human body that has no blood supply is the cornea in the **eye**. It takes in oxygen directly from the air.

Four is the only number in the English language that has the same number of letters in its name as its meaning.

More than 2,500 cover versions of The Beatles' "Yesterday" exist, making it the most recorded song in history.
Apart from 'The Frog Chorus'.

Dracula (**Draclia**) is the most filmed story of all time.

Maine is the **only** state in the United States whose name is just one syllable.

The only active diamond mine in the United States is in Arkansas.

Chancery Lane has the *shortest* escalator on the London Underground system – only 50 steps.

Teeth are the only parts of the human body that **can't** repair themselves.

Mickey Mouse has four fingers on each hand.

Zara Phillips got her Christian name from her uncle, **Prince Charles**. He thought that Zara, a Greek biblical name, which meant 'bright as the dawn' was apt for such a bright baby. His sister, **Princess Anne**, clearly thought that Charles had good judgement.

After **Rod Stewart**'s wife **Rachel Hunter** left him in 1999, the in-his-60s singer announced that he couldn't carry on chasing young girls. He soon turned up with **Penny Lancaster** – aged 28.

Ex-Spice Girl Geri Halliwell claims to plunge into a freezing cold bath for five minutes every morning to help tone her skin and prevent her ever needing a face lift!

Leonardo DiCaprio had to lose a stone and a half in just two weeks for his role in *The Beach*.

Liz Hurley and **Hugh Grant**'s production company, Simian Films, got its name from Liz's belief that Hugh has monkey-like features.

Singer **Anastacia** and actor **Jeff Hordley**, who plays Cain Dingle in *Emmerdale*, both suffer from the bowel disorder Crohn's disease.

Phoenix Nights star **Peter Kay** was taught metalwork at school by **Steve Coogan**'s dad. *Knowing Me, Knowing Metalwork.*

Although he grew up in Australia and still has a strong Aussie accent, **Peter Andre** was actually born in London.

Before joining *EastEnders* as Chrissie Watts, **Tracy-Ann Oberman** appeared in nearly 600 plays for Radio 4.

The tune hummed by **David Brent** during his infamous dance routine in *The Office* was "Disco Inferno", a track used in *Saturday Night Fever*. *Can you dig it? I knew that you could.*

Keanu Reeves was not first choice for the role of Neo in *The Matrix*. He was only offered the part after it had been rejected by **Ewan McGregor**.

Tony Blair is a distant cousin of the **Queen**.

Countdown babe **Carol Vorderman** has an IQ of 154.

Before marrying **Prince Edward**, **Sophie Rhys-Jones** dated Michael Parkinson's **son**.

The letter 'T' in *Star Trek*'s **Captain James T. Kirk**'s name stands for Tiberius.

To help create the special effects seen in *Star Trek*, several different models of the Enterprise were made. They ranged in size between fourteen feet and three inches.

Trying to fly them is not recommended.

Actress **Keira Knightley** is dyslexic and had to wear special glasses during adolescence to help her read.

Welsh singing star Charlotte Church made her stage debut aged three and a half. She performed 'Ghostbusters' with her cousin at a holiday camp in Caernarfon.

Pop guru **Louis Walsh** managed his first band – Time Machine – at the age of 15.

A school teacher once asked a young **Justin Timberlake** whether he would prefer to be a famous name in either music or basketball. He said basketball.

Ulrika Jonsson once licked a lamppost when she was a child in Sweden and got stuck. It took three friends blowing warm air to loosen her tongue's grip on the pole.

Actor **Ralf Little** was planning a career in medicine, and studying for A-levels, when he landed a role in *The Royle Family*.

As a child, **Catherine Zeta Jones** was exposed to a virus that gave her breathing difficulties. She had tracheotomy surgery, which has left her with a scar on her neck.

Al Pacino is the same height as **Dustin Hoffman**.

Penelope Cruz is a collector of coat hangers.

Doctor Who was so popular during the 1960s that The Beatles wanted to make an appearance in the show. A scene was written into an episode in which they appeared on the Time and Space Visualiser, which was depicting a **Beatles** fiftieth-anniversary concert in 2015, with the Fab Four dressed up as old men. The group themselves were interested in the idea, but it was vetoed by their manager, **Brian Epstein**, and never recorded.

Uma Thurman's father was the first ever American citizen to be ordained as a buddhist monk.

Kim Cattrall was born Clare Woodgate.

When *EastEnders*' **Joe Swash** was seven, he made his first TV appearance in a classic Andrex advert. He was the little boy who wiped off his grandmother's slobbery kiss.

Rowan Atkinson's luxury item on the radio programme *Desert Island Discs* was a car to clean.

Before hitting the big time with *Little Britain*, **David Walliams** used to be a script writer for **Ant and Dec**.

Johnny Depp is scared of clowns.

Natasha and **Daniel Bedingfield** are the only brother and sister to have had separate solo number one hits in the UK.

Woody Allen, **Kevin Costner**, **Warren Beatty**, **Robert Redford** and **Mel Gibson** have all won Oscars for Best Director, but never for Best Actor.

Cindy Crawford was the first modern supermodel to pose for *Playboy*.

CAUTION. HEAVY PLANT CROSSING

American actor **Rick Moranis** had to speak and act slowly in *Little Shop of Horrors* as scenes involving the carnivorous alien plant Audrey II had to be shot slowly so that it moved convincingly. *Caution: plant crossing.*

Ex-boxer **Chris Eubank**'s trademark gold monocle was once stolen as he helped a sick passenger on a train.

Tony Blair claimed his favourite pop song was "The House of the Rising Sun" by **The Animals** when he appeared on *Top of the Pops. Tony didn't actually perform but he did offer up his rendition of The Stranglers classic* **"Gordon Brown**, *just like the last."*

Before becoming a singing star, **Daniel Bedingfield** used to work as a web designer for Teletext.

57 per cent of British schoolkids think Germany is the most **boring** country in Europe.

Monkey wrench is a cocktail made of white rum, grapefruit juice and lemon juice. *It was also the weapon used to kill Tommy Harris in* **Coronation Street**.

A biggin is a plain close-fitting cap, often tied under the chin and popular in the 16th and 17th centuries. *Christopher Biggins was in fact named after them.*

A branch of the Germanic royal family changed its name from **Battenberg** to Mountbatten.
But the cake stayed loyal.

The pop group **Duran Duran** took their name from a character in the science fiction film *Barbarella*.
Girls Aloud didn't.

Mary Queen of Scots wrote letters to her supporters in **invisible** ink while she was in prison awaiting execution.
Here's one of them ...

Fascinating!

Bucks Fizz is a cocktail of champagne and orange juice. Grenadine is an optional extra, but before ordering think about whether you want it. *"Making Your Mind Up" really.*

The white part of your fingernail is called the **lunula**.
The black part is called grime.

If you get a stitch on your right side while running, try to exhale as your left foot hits the ground. And vice versa.
Best not to go running in the first place.

Protesters in Australia wrote "Howard's End" on their backsides and then mooned at Prime Minister John Howard. *Just for a moment, you thought they were writing a movie on their arses, didn't you?*

I'm getting something ... wait ... yes ... I hear you ... The **Ouija** board is named from the French and German words for yes: "oui" and "ja".

If you yelled for 8 years, 7 months and 6 days you would produce enough sound **energy** to heat one cup of coffee. *Hardly seems worth it, does it?*

Violet Carson, who played Ena Sharples in *Coronation Street* for **20** years, was a pianist accompanying silent films before becoming an actress.

You're more likely to divorce or move house than *change* **your bank.**

National Service for men of 18 was started in this country in 1947 and **abolished** in 1963.

The pupils at the centre of a goat's eyes are **square**.

So are the pupils of Eton.

Scientist Isaac Newton invented **the cat flap.**

The Caesar family has two months named after them. July was named for Julius Caesar and August for Augustus Caesar.

And of course they used to say "Hail, Caesar" when it was raining.

Prostitutes in Romania suspended their services for **Lent**.

When St Paul's Cathedral was being built and the money to pay for it was running out, architect Christopher Wren got himself **elected** as an MP and tripled the tax that was paying for it.

The number of people **smoking** in Britain has fallen from 50 per cent in the 1950s to about 27 per cent today.

Water expands by about 10% as it freezes.

A pangram is a sentence that contains all 26 letters of the English alphabet. For example:
Pac*k* *my* **b**o**x** w*it***h** *fi*v**e** **d**oz*en* l*i***q**uo**r** j**u**g*s*.

Snails can sleep for three years without eating.

Tea was rationed to two **ounces** a week during the Second World War.

"Rhythms" is the longest English word without vowels.

The type of **sandwich** filling you choose tells a lot about you, say experts. BLT means you're hard-working and self-motivated while tuna and cucumber indicates you're caring and giving. *Cheese and tomato suggests you're in plumbing or welding, and Spam and curried bean indicates a propensity toward Chavness.*

"Freelance" originally meant mercenary soldier, a person who was free to use his lance for you, if you had **money** to pay him.

Pigs and humans are the only creatures that get sunburnt.

Swedish legislator Lars Gustafsson once nominated **football** for the Nobel Peace Prize because it helps promote good international relations.

"swims"

is the longest word with 180-degree rotational symmetry – if you were to view it upside-down it would still be the same word and perfectly readable.

"swims"

The immensely **talented** Lesley Douglas, Controller of BBC Radio 2, was voted the music industry's Woman of the Year 2004 for the continued success of the nation's favourite radio station, and for her sterling work running it. *We believe Douglas, the capital of the Isle of Man, is in fact named after her descendants.*

Ely is the English city with the *shortest* number of letters in its name.

More than 1,000 people **trekked** 31 miles through the Channel Tunnel for charity when it was completed in 1994. They were the first people to walk from Britain to France since the Ice Age.

Scientist Galileo was placed under house arrest for nine years for saying the Earth went round the sun. He escaped torture and execution by renouncing his findings.

The colour combination with the **strongest** visual impact is black and yellow.

A "**Blue Moon**" is the second full moon in a calendar month, but it's rarely blue.

An Australian couple called their children Kitchen, Bathroom, and Garage after the rooms they were conceived in.

The only countries in the world outside of the UK with **one** syllable in their names are Chad, France, Greece, and Spain. *Go on – prove us a wrong. The winner gets a sixpence.*

Clement Attlee, who was responsible for the foundation of the welfare state after World War Two, was voted the most successful British prime minister of all time by experts in History and Politics. Churchill came *second*.

Shopkeeper F W Woolworth opened his first "five and ten cent store" in Utica, New York, in 1879. *It's due for a refit next week.*

If you perform hongi in New Zealand you greet someone by **rubbing** noses.

The **football** club Sheffield Wednesday was founded by a group of shop workers on their afternoon off.

A phalacrosis sufferer loses their hair.
Here's my drawing of my radio show co-host Tim Smith.

French playwright Molière **died** on stage while playing an ill man. *The audience thought the violent coughing fit that killed him was a particularly fine performance.*

Christopher Eccleston is the first actor to play Doctor Who to be born after the show first began in November 1963. *What a coincidence to be born right after the show! Oh … I see …*

Britney Spears needed four stitches after a heavy camera fell on her during the filming of the video for 'Oops! I did it again'. *The camera also needed major repairs.*

Heather Mills McCartney was nominated for the Nobel Peace Prize in 1996.

Billie Piper's middle name is Paul.

When she was 17, model **Rachel Hunter** was asked to pose for *Playboy*. She felt she was too young at the time so she turned the offer down. In 2004, she was asked again. This time she felt she was old enough and was paid $1.8 million for the privilege.

British TV actress **Amanda Holden** had her acting break in 1985 in an episode of *EastEnders* playing a stallholder called Carmen. She has said that the day she left Walford, she slipped a note under the producer's door suggesting Carmen should come back and that the audience should learn her surname is "Getme".

Before hitting the big time with *The Office*, **Ricky Gervais** used to manage Indie-band **Suede**.

Davina McCall and husband-to-be Matthew Robertson got so engrossed when they shared their first kiss that they got locked inside a park.

Before finding fame with **Girls Aloud**, singer **Sarah Harding** worked as a pizza girl whilst fellow bandmate **Cheryl Tweedy** earned a living as a cocktail waitress.

Debra Messing beat *Desperate Housewives* star
Nicollette Sheridan (aka man-eater Edie
Britt) for the role of Grace Adler in *Will & Grace* at the
final auditions.

Formerly curvy model **Sophie Dahl** was the
inspiration for the character of Sophie in her
grandfather **Roald Dahl**'s famous novel *The BFG*.

Westlife star **Shane Filan** has installed a
state-of-the-art security system at his Irish
mansion, which allows him to view all the rooms
in his house from wherever he is in the world.

Derek Martin had several chances to appear in *EastEnders* before joining the cast as Charlie Slater. He turned down the role of Frank Butcher and even auditioned for the part of Den Watts.

Superstitious **Dermot O'Leary** kisses the window before he goes to bed each night. *That sounds like a compulsive disorder to me.*

Former *EastEnders* actor **Jack Ryder**'s father is **Jack Hues**, who fronted Eighties band **Wang Chung**.

When she was growing up, **Victoria Beckham** didn't like being driven to school in her father's Rolls Royce because she was worried about what people would think. Now husband **David Beckham** owns a fleet of luxury cars.

Heat magazine's biggest selling cover star ever is **Jade Goody**.

At the age of eleven **Beyoncé Knowles** recorded her life ambitions on a camcorder. On the tape she said she wanted to record a gold album, which she would follow up with a platinum-selling second album, with a third which she wanted to both write and produce. She achieved all these ambitions by the time she was 21 years old.

Before landing the role of Tanya Turner in *Footballers' Wives*, actress **Zöe Lucker** was about to give up acting for a career as a teacher.

Alan Davies wore his own duffel coat in all the early episodes of *Jonathan Creek*.

George W Bush is only the second president to follow in his father's footsteps. The first father-and-son presidents were **John Adams** and **John Quincy Adams**.

Pete Waterman used to own the famous train *The Flying Scotsman*.

When she was seven years old, *Coronation Street*'s Shelley, actress **Sally Lindsay**, had a number one hit. She was a member of the St Winifred's School Choir which topped the charts with "There's no one quite like Grandma".

When **Kylie Minogue** launched her own range of Kylie dolls a 3-D scanning device was used to create a mould of her face.

Actor **James Alexandrou**, who plays Martin Fowler in *EastEnders*, used to swim for his county, and was once ranked in the top 10 in the country for his age.

Whilst working as a freelance home economist during the 1960s, top singer and cook **Delia Smith** made the garish cake which appears on the front cover of the Rolling Stones' album *Let it Bleed*.

The 24-hour clock was not used in the **Kiefer Sutherland** drama *24* because it is not frequently referred to in the USA, with many Americans not sure of how it works.

Supermodel Elle McPherson was known as The Body because her dimensions of 36-24-35 are considered perfect.

When **Jack Nicholson** was 37 he discovered that his sister was actually his mother.

The leg on the poster for the **Dustin Hoffman** film *The Graduate* is not that of co-star the late **Anne Bancroft**, but of fellow actress **Linda Gray**, who went on to find fame as Sue Ellen in *Dallas*. *"A tramp, a drunk and an unfit mother – as soon as we can get you into that Sanitorium, the better Sue Ellen."*

Actress **Kate Winslet** has had a street named after her in her hometown of Reading. The cul de sac of fifty houses is known as 'Winslet Place'.

Welsh singing starlet **Charlotte Church** turned down a role in the movie version of **Andrew Lloyd Webber**'s *Phantom Of The Opera* – because the film-makers wanted her to lose weight.

Despite their debut single "Sound of the Underground" selling 213,000 copies in its first week, and remaining at number one for several weeks, the members of **Girls Aloud** received just £6,000 each from sales of the record.

Denise van Outen was actually born Denise Outen, but later added the "van" to make it sound more interesting, *not because she was born in a van.*

During her first screen test for *Sky Sports*, **Kirsty Gallacher** messed up her lines and was offered a job as a tea girl.

Although she is half-Ecuadorian and has released a Spanish album, **Christina Aguilera** hardly speaks a word of Spanish. *Don't know which half.*

Long before he began campaigning for better school dinners, **Jamie Oliver** was asked by **Tony Blair** to become an official "food tsar" for hospitals. Oliver declined.

Seal popped the question to supermodel **Heidi Klum** after taking her 10,000 feet up a mountain in Canada and into an igloo that he had built himself.

Pamela Anderson was known as "rubber-band" at school because she was so athletic.
Athletic – yup – that's undeniable.

Before becoming a musical star and so-called serial love rat, **Darren Day** was a semi-professional snooker player.

Tony Blair once ran away from his school. One housemaster called him "the most difficult boy I ever had to deal with". *No change there then.*

Newlyweds star **Jessica Simpson** used to leave notes on her mirror telling herself how beautiful she was.

Coronation Street's Sarah Louise Platt, actress **Tina O'Brien**, is known as Teeny Tina by her friends and family because she is so small.

Model **Nell McAndrew**'s real
Christian name is Tracy.

Jennifer Lopez was the first Hispanic actress to
earn more than $1 million a film.

"Corrie" actress **Jane Danson**, who plays Leanne
Battersby, was crowned Rosebud Queen of the Morris Dancing
Team when she was ten years old.

Fame Academy singing coach **Carrie Grant** once
represented the UK in the Eurovision song contest.

US President George W Bush gave up alcohol on his
40th birthday. *It is believed his wife had given him an
ultimatum – it was either her or Jack Daniels.*

In the annual Festival of Women, held in parts of Greece, **men** stay at home, clean the house, feed the children and do the washing, while the women spend the day playing backgammon and telling stories.

Elvis Presley's US Army number was 53310761.

A cathedral is a church that contains a cathedra, or **throne** of the bishop of the diocese.

A Canadian woman discovered smoking was dangerous when she sneaked out of a Winnipeg hospital for a fag. Staff didn't see her go and locked her out in freezing temperatures.

Our eyes are the same size from birth but our ears and nose never stop gro**wing**.

The working title for the TV series *Drop The Dead Donkey* was 'Dead Belgians Don't Count'.

Billy Foulke was the heaviest footballer to play for England. A goalkeeper, he weighed 22 stone and used to pick up strikers who annoyed him by the ankles and bounce them in the mud.

A weather centre in Aberdeen and a tide gauge in Portsmouth were the only reported victims of the Millennium Bug in Britain.

"You've Lost That Lovin' Feeling" was unanimously voted a miss on *Juke Box Jury* in 1965 and one of the panellists even questioned whether it was being played at the right speed.

Sean Connery's **first** film was *Lilacs in the Spring* in 1954.

Ronald Reagan's **last** film was *The Killers* in 1964.

The first British telephone directory, published in 1880, had 25 names in it.

The farm where Constable painted his *Hay Wain* belonged to Willie Lott.

No word in the English language rhymes with the word "month".

Polaris, the pole star, is 680 light years from Earth.

Although Frankie Dettori won all seven races in a day at Ascot, former champion jockey Sir Gordon Richards once had *12 consecutive winners*, one at Nottingham, all six the next day at Chepstow, and the first five the following day.

In April 2005, councillors said owners of horses which roam free through the streets of Cardiff could be given **ASBO**s, after shoppers at a 24-hour supermarket were left *shocked* when a Shetland pony walked into a store in Pengam Green in Cardiff and began wandering the aisles.

Why the long face?

An 86-year-old great-grandfather from the Wirral was served with an **Anti-social behaviour order** after constantly *banging* his garage door and dustbin lids. *He's now been asked to join the cast of* Stomp.

Age is no barrier. One 10-year-old in Bath, who caused £80,000 of **arson** damage, is banned from having matches until he turns 16.

Bath magistrates served an **ASBO** on a young woman, preventing her from jumping into rivers, canals or on to railway lines, following four suicide bids. *Well, that's going to deter her ...*

An Eastbourne man who's old enough to know **better** was banned for five years from sunbathing naked or in a thong.

In the first **ASBO** of its kind, an Eminem and Dido fan from Birmingham who incessantly played the musicians' songs at top volume was *banned* from owning a stereo, radio or TV.

A Wirral family of five's **ASBO** prohibits them from "*harassing* anyone in England and Wales" . . . *So they're not allowed to talk to anyone?*

Taxi drivers in North Wales have been *warned* that if they repeatedly beep their horn as they pick up customers, they may be served with an **Anti-social behaviour order**. A police letter was sent out to cabbies calling on them to end the practice.

A family feud led to a woman from North Yorkshire being given an **ASBO** for *attacking* her brother with:

a) a shoe

b) a stick of rhubarb

c) malice aforethought

[Answer: b) a stick of rhubarb. Wonder what the feud was over: probably just some old manure.]

Wearing a woolly hat, baseball cap or *hooded* top now comes with unusual risks for a 21-year-old from Teesside, after he had an **ASBO** slapped on him for sporting the headgear.

Knocking on the front door of any home in Britain could now land a 30-year-old Londoner in jail. The man's **ASBO** also extended to *banning* him from using doorbells or phoning households without permission.

A young man from Scotland who is obsessed with the film *An American Werewolf in London* was jailed for four months after breaching an **ASBO** which banned his persistent howling.

In London a barrister was served with an **ASBO** after noisily *banging* her mop against her floors and walls.

An **ASBO** *banning* him from all NHS buildings in the country was handed to a man in York with a fetish for medical supplies, after he tried to get hold of surgical masks on 47 occasions in 2004. *Also, a skellington went missing.*

On the Wirral, a man was banned from assaulting and *verbally* abusing bin men after they were so intimidated by his behaviour that they stopped collecting rubbish from his street. *Intimidating dustmen? Personally, I find that hard to believe...*

In Liverpool, a 51-year-old with 35 drunk and *disorderly* convictions has been told he could get five years in jail if he is found drunk anywhere on Merseyside.

The most common time for a bank **robbery** is Friday between 9 and 11am. The least likely time is Wednesday between 3 and 6pm. *So it wouldn't be me because I'm on the air most of that time.*

A Zambian man divorced his wife after he found a frog in a cup of tea she gave him.

What they didn't know was that it was in fact a handsome prince.

The average British **mobile** telephone bill is £20 a month. *Not if you've got a 19-year-old son.*

The biggest frog in the world unusually has a human name. Dubbed **Keith Baxter**, he lives under a slab in Yeovil, Somerset.

The word "budget" comes from the French "bougette", meaning "little bag" – which explains why the Chancellor "opens" his budget.

Queen Victoria sent over 2,500 **Valentine** cards during her reign. *She was amused.*

The first **text** message was sent in 1992. *I've just received it, I'll be replying in a moment – as soon as I can get the predictive text off...*

In Cyprus, it is sunny for approximately 360 days of the year.

Only three grape varieties can be used in **champagne** – Chardonnay, Pinot Noir and Pinot Meuniere. The latter has never been grown successfully anywhere in the world outside the Champagne region.

Women were asked by the Government during the Second World War to save wood by having flatter shoes.

The reason you don't laugh when you tickle yourself is that the **brain** anticipates and disregards your own touch so it can focus on anticipating unexpected sensations – *such as polishing with Cillit Bang.*

More than one million copies of the 2005 J. K. Rowling book *Harry Potter and the Half-Blood Prince* **were sold before it was even published.**

When the Queen visited the Sultan of Brunei she was issued with an **etiquette** list which included not wearing yellow, not pointing and not sneezing in public.

The average bed is home to over **6 billion** dust mites. *Who's counted them, then?*

Human **thigh** bones are stronger than concrete.

A duck's quack doesn't echo, and nobody knows why.

The first CD pressed in America was **Bruce Springsteen**'s *Born in the USA*.

The most expensive spice in the world is saffron... *I thought it was* **Victoria Beckham**.

Bruce Lee was so fast that they actually had to **s-l-o-w** film down so you could see his moves.

If you place a tiny amount of alcohol on a scorpion, it will instantly go mad and sting itself to death... *Which sadist discovered this?*

When Action Man got a makeover he was given Russell Crowe's mouth, David Beckham's nose, Brad Pitt's jaw, Tom Cruise's hair ... *and Van Morrison's personality.*

Humans and dolphins are the only species that have sex for pleasure.

"A man a plan a canal panama"
spelled backwards is still
"A man a plan a canal panama"
This factoid is amongst my top ten favourite ever factoids.

Did you know that an **anagram** of "ELEVEN PLUS TWO" is "TWELVE PLUS ONE"? ... *Freaky or what?*

A **badger** sett has between 3 and 10 entrances ...
Hi honey, I'm home ...

It's a factoid that all domestic cats hate lemons, or any citrus scent of any kind.

147

SEX SE

JUST A

Coffee drinkers have sex more frequently and enjoy it more than non-coffee drinkers.

CTION 2

QUICKIE

Moose intercourse typically lasts about five seconds.

Thurrock Council in Essex ordered smoking workers to put in an **extra** half hour a day to compensate for time lost on cigarette breaks.

Did you know – porcupines **float** in water?

US President George W Bush has one of his minions download music for him and he listens to his **iPod** while mountain-biking. He's a fan of country music and classic rock, but he also likes "a little bit of hard core and honky tonk".

Alexander Graham Bell, the inventor of the telephone, never telephoned his wife or mother because they were both **deaf**.

A person breathes **seven** quarts of air every minute.

From BBC TV comedy *Little Britain*,
"*I'm the only gay in the village!*"
was voted top TV catchphrase in
a poll conducted by UKTV Gold.
Other *Little Britain* phrases
"*Yeah but … no but*" and
"*I'm a lady*" were also in the
top 20. Tommy Cooper's "*Just
Like That*" and Homer Simpson's
"*Doh!*" were second and third.

The **Crazy Frog** was the first mobile phone ringtone to top the charts, and its rise to the top proved that yoofs spend more money on mobile phones and computer games than music.

The middle day of a non-leap year is July 2.

Each king in a deck of playing cards represents a great king from history: Spades = King David; Clubs = Alexander the Great; Hearts = Charlemagne; and Diamonds = Julius Caesar.

To click a mouse burns 0.0000024kcals of energy, so if you eat a chocolate bar you'll need to click your mouse 765,551,000 times to burn it off. *Good luck on that.*

In the summer of 2005, the average rainfall for the whole of June fell during seven hours on the **Glastonbury Festival**, and the fire brigade had to pump three million litres of water off the site.

Western outlaw Wild Bill Hickok was killed playing poker, holding two pairs – aces and eights – which has become known as "Dead Man's Hand". *P.S. When we say "Western", we don't mean Truro.*

Two US presidents died on the same day: John Adams and Thomas Jefferson both died on July 4, 1826.

On average, right-handed people live 9 years longer than their left-handed counterparts.

Only **one** in two billion people will live to be 116 or older.

95% of all text messages are delivered within 10 seconds.
Not necessarily on my phone.

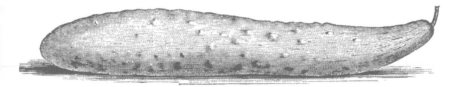

96% of the weight of a cucumber is water.

Our nails grow at a rate of around **0.1mm** per day. So it takes roughly three months to replace an entire fingernail.

There are 333 sheets on the average toilet-paper roll.

DNA stands for DeoxyriboNucleicAcid.

To humans, acorns are **poisonous** and if digested can cause kidney damage.

A man died in Hereford in June at the age of 105 just after celebrating his *80th* wedding anniversary. He and his wife were officially the longest surviving married couple in Britain.

New York's murder rate has fallen from 2,245 in 1990 to about 500 in the last year thanks, it's believed, to so-called **"zero tolerance"** policing.

A piece of string is twice as long as half its length . . . *I've no idea what that means. You work it out, I'm writing this and it's 11.30 at night.*

Leonardo da Vinci could write with one hand whilst drawing with the other. *Not impressed? Then you try it. Oh, and he was also mopping the floor with his feet at the same time too.*

Barbie's measurements, if she were life size, would be 39-23-33.

A shark's 'skellington' is made of cartilage – it has no bone.

Half of all teenage boys say they would rather be rich than clever.

Moths can't eat because they have neither mouths nor stomachs. *No wonder they're so thin – they need a good meal. Light bulbs are no good for 'em.*

The human body contains enough **fat** to make seven bars of soap. *Unless it's Pavarotti, then it's 31.*

85% of red lingerie is purchased by men.
Yet you hardly ever see them wear it.

Charles Dickens always wrote facing north.
Surely that's not a book title?

Guess how many cheques will be deducted from the wrong bank accounts in the next hour? Your options are:

    a) 2,000

    b) 12,000

    c) 22,000

[Answer: incredibly, it's c) 22,000! (If you wish to complain, press 2 now....)]

The Romans were very fond of eating dormice. *In fact, Dormouse Wellington was immensely popular, with or without fur.*

China has the largest donkey population in the world, but how many do current estimates say there are?

    a) 8 million

    b) 11 million

    c) 14 million

[Answer: the world's top donkey-counters think it's b) 11 million. That's one for every 100 Chinamen – or women.]

Blonde beards grow quicker than dark beards. *But not on women.*

It's estimated that at any one time, 0.7 per cent of the world's population are drunk.

In your car, 51 per cent of turns are right turns.

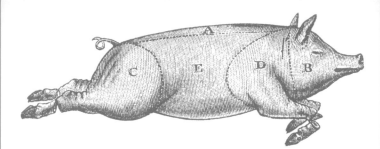

Hog is a generic name for all swine – so a pig is a hog but a hog is not necessarily a pig.
Janey Lee Grace

One superstition to get rid of **warts** is to rub them with a peeled apple and then feed the apple to a pig.
Tim Smith

The art of map-making is older than the art of writing.
Miles Mendoza

According to the ancient Chinese, swinging your arms **cures** headaches.
Old Woman

The word "sheriff" comes from "shire reeve". In feudal England each shire had a reeve who upheld the law for that shire.
Miles Mendoza

The terrac, a Madagascan insectivore,
has 22 to 24 **nipples**.
Janey Lee Grace

Purple is by far the **favourite** ink colour in pens
used by bingo players.
Old Woman

Tablecloths were originally used as towels on which dinner
guests could **wipe** their hands and faces after eating.
Tim Smith

A chamois goat can balance on a **point** of rock the size of a £1 coin.

Tim Smith

A grasshopper needs a minimum air temperature of 62 degrees Fahrenheit before it's able to **hop**.

Tim Smith

Some toothpaste contains crushed volcanic stone.

Tim Smith

Cows and horses sleep standing up.

Old Woman

Taramasalata, a type of Greek salad, and Galatasaray, a Turkish football club, each has an "**A**" for every other letter.

Tim Smith

Snakes **hear** through their jaws.

Janey Lee Grace

Rabbits have been known to reach a speed of 47mph.

Janey Lee Grace

Beaver teeth are so **sharp** that Native Americans once used them as knife blades.

Old Woman

English soldiers of the Hundred Years' War were known to the French as "**Les Goddamns**" because of their propensity to swear.

Janey Lee Grace

Acknowledgements

Steve:

Thank you to our trusted co-editor Chris Smith, to Hannah
Warner for her Reality TV contribution, to all the listeners to
Steve Wright in the Afternoon whose thirst for trivia inspired this
book, to my son Tom and daughter Lucy for their factoids
which I've snuck in somewhere in the middle, and thank you
to the BBC for letting me impart all this crucial info on my
radio programme on BBC Radio 2, which by the way, starts at
2 o'clock every afternoon.

Jessica:

As Wrighty does the jokes, Friend, I'd just like to add . . . for
their help and support with the book – very special thanks and
much love to Tony, Frances and William Rickson, and further
thanks and love to my friends, including those at Radio 2.

Picture Acknowledgements

And a special big thank you to all our friends at Rex Features,
for their help in supplying all the photos used in this book.